ANIMAL VS ANIMAL

WHO'S THE
DEADLIEST?

BY KIRSTY HOLMES

BookLife PUBLISHING

©2019
BookLife Publishing
King's Lynn
Norfolk PE30 4LS

All rights reserved.
Printed in Malaysia.

A catalogue record for this book is available from the British Library.

ISBN: 978-1-78637-520-9

Written by:
Kirsty Holmes

Edited by:
Robin Twiddy

Designed by:
Danielle Rippengill

All facts, statistics, web addresses and URLs in this book were verified as valid and accurate at time of writing. No responsibility for any changes to external websites or references can be accepted by either the author or publisher.

IMAGE CREDITS

All images are courtesy of Shutterstock.com, unless otherwise specified. With thanks to Getty Images, Thinkstock Photo and iStockphoto. Cover – Ovocheva, Stepova Oksana, Abscent, Maquiladora. Images used on every page – Ovocheva, Stepova Oksana. 5 – ONYXprj, Abscent. 6&7 – Guingm. 7 – Maquiladora, VectorShow. 8 – Kerry Matz National Institute of General Medical Services. 9 – reptiles4all. 8&9 – Guingm. 10&11 – Abscent, venimo, ASAG Studio. 12 – Dewald Kirsten. 13 – NickEvansKZN. 12&13 – Guingm. 14&15 – Abscent. 16 – Tim Ezzy. 17 – Ondrej Prosicky, Maquiladora. 16&17 – Guingm. 18 – VectorShow. 19 – Maquiladora. 18&19 – Abscent. 20&21 – amiloslava. 22 – Guingm. 23 – Abscent.

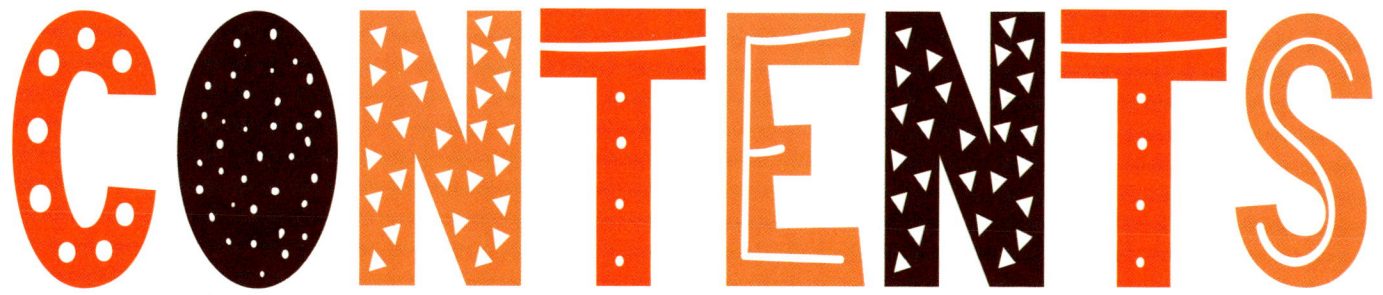

PAGE 4	The Great and Small Games
PAGE 6	The Contenders
PAGE 8	Cone Snail vs Poison Dart Frog
PAGE 10	The Poison-O-Meter
PAGE 12	Box Jellyfish vs Black Mamba
PAGE 14	Target Terror
PAGE 16	Saltwater Crocodile vs Hippopotamus
PAGE 18	Bite Club
PAGE 20	Hall of Fame
PAGE 22	Quiz and Activity
PAGE 24	Glossary and Index

Words that look like **this** can be found in the glossary on page 24.

THE GREAT AND SMALL GAMES

Roll Up! Roll Up!
It's the Great and Small Games!
See nature's darkest and deadliest creatures in action!

Today's events:
The Poison-O-Meter!
Target Terror!
Bite Club!

These events will surely decide once and for all:
Who's the Deadliest?

THE CONTENDERS

"Let's find out some facts and figures about today's contenders!"

Golden Poison Dart Frog
Little but Lethal

Size: Up to 55 millimetres (mm)

Lives: Colombia, South America

Weapon: Skin

Geographer Cone Snail
The Silent Assassin

Size: Up to 15 centimetres (cm)

Lives: Reefs in the Indo-Pacific Ocean

Weapon: Harpoon

Box Jellyfish
The Tentacles of Doom

Size: Up to 3 metres (m)

Lives: Coasts of Northern Australia and the Indo-Pacific

Weapon: Tentacles

6

Black Mamba
The Mouth of Midnight

Size: Around 4 m

Lives: Southern and Eastern Africa

Weapon: Lethal venom

Hippopotamus
The Muddy Maniac

Size: Around 1,300 kilograms (kg)

Lives: Sub-Saharan Africa

Weapon: Strong bite force and sharp teeth

Saltwater Crocodile
The Jaws of Death

Size: Around 5–6 m

Lives: Eastern India, Southeast Asia, and Northern Australia

Weapon: Strong bite force and sharp teeth

CONE SNAIL VS

I'm so pretty!

Rrrrrrround Onnnne!

Just one sting from this gruesome **gastropod** can instantly **paralyse** its prey. Armed with a poisoned harpoon and able to swallow prey whole, this snail's shell may be pretty, but remember... looks can kill.

Nickname:
The Silent Assassin

Fatal Facts:
Cone snails can make a **toxin** designed for each prey.

POISON DART FROG

Hopping in from South America, this tiny terror might look beautiful – but its effects are anything but! This rainbow reptile's skin holds a deadly toxin strong enough to kill TWO African bull elephants!

Nickname:
Little but Lethal

Fatal Facts:
Poison dart frogs have been used for centuries to make poison arrows by local **indigenous people**.

Their bright colours tell <u>predators</u> that they are poisonous.

CROAK!

THE POISON-O-METER

The Poison-O-Meter measures how many mice each creature could kill with a single dose of poison. Contenders must add 1 milligram (mg) of poison into the poison-o-meter. The most mice wins!

First up: the geographer cone snail...

There are 800 **species** of cone snail, and each can make hundreds of toxins! Just like having a chemistry set inside them!

10,000
7,500
5,000
2,500
0

Poison: 1 mg

Total Mice: 1,600

Now for our **second contender:** the golden poison dart frog.

Poison: 1 mg

Total Mice: 10,000

One frog carries enough poison to kill 10 adult humans!

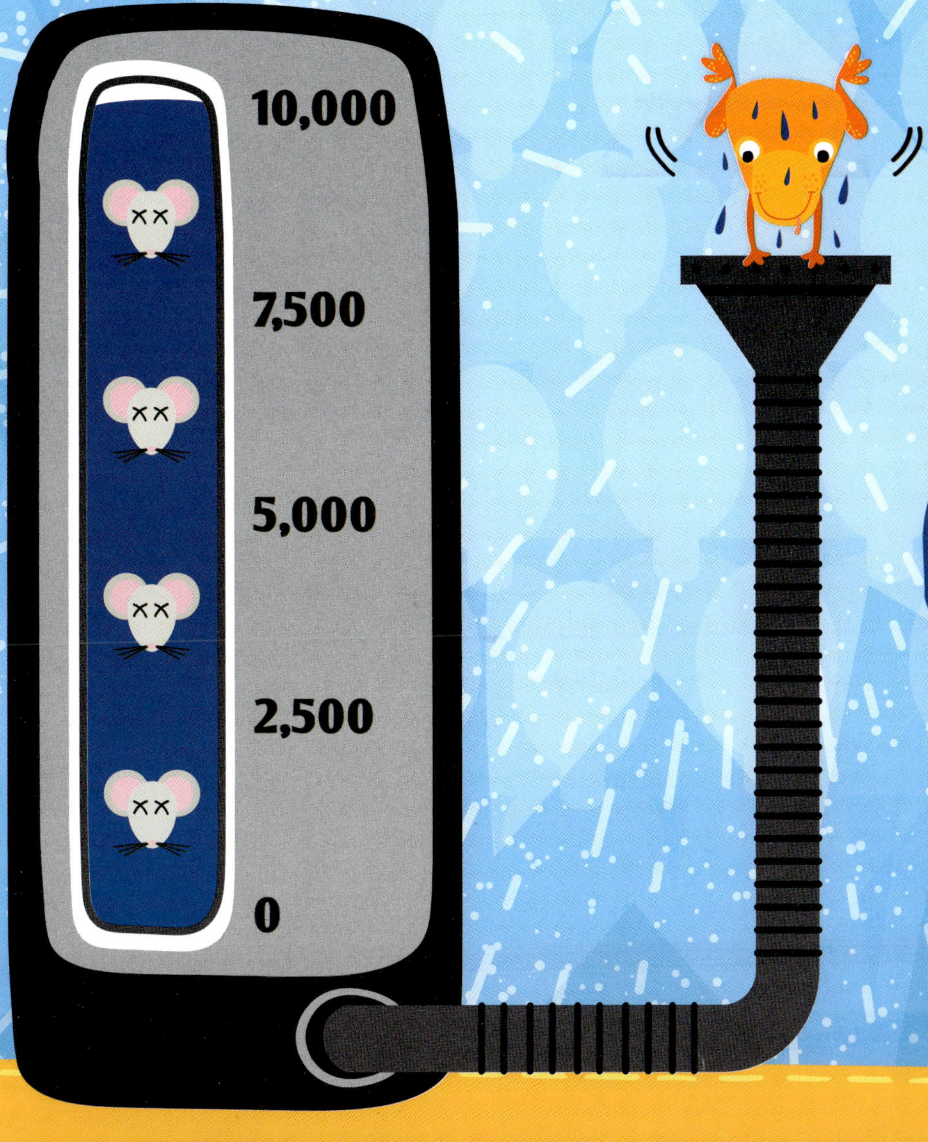

10,000
7,500
5,000
2,500
0

Round one goes to the **poison dart frog!**

BOX JELLYFISH VS

Rrrrrrround Twoooo!

The box jellyfish is known as the Sucker Punch of the Sea – it's almost invisible, and you'll barely feel its sting... But you'll know about it soon afterwards! Once you've been stung, tiny capsules pump the venom into your blood... and death can follow quickly after.

Nickname:
The Tentacles of Doom

Fatal Facts:
Some people say to pee on a jellyfish sting – but don't!

BLACK MAMBA

With her coffin-shaped head and terrifying black mouth, this is one seriously scary serpent! In South Africa, her bite is known as the kiss of death, and she can deliver up to 400 mg of venom in one single snap!

Nickname:
The Mouth of Midnight

Fatal Facts:
If not treated with **antivenom**, the black mamba bite can kill a grown human in 7–15 hours.

HISSSS!

Black mambas aren't actually black – they are olive green.

TARGET TERROR

Venomous animals deliver their poison directly – through stings, bites, or harpoons. We're going to look at two deadly delivery methods by testing their targeting skills.

Box jellyfish are known as sea wasps.

Aim: ☠☠
Speed: ☠☠
Venom: ☠☠☠☠☠
Total: 9

Our **second** contender: the black mamba.

Aim: 💀💀💀💀💀
Speed: 💀💀💀💀💀
Venom: 💀💀💀💀💀
Total: 15

They get their name from their scary black mouths!

Round two goes to the **black mamba!**

SALTWATER CROCODILE

Rrrrrrround Threee!

SNAP! SNAP!

The largest living reptile, and known to his friends as the saltie, this **marine** crocodile has a mouth full of razor-sharp teeth and a tiny brain. But don't call him stupid – he might just eat you up!

Nickname:
The Jaws of Death

Fatal Facts:
Since 1976, 106 people are believed to have been killed by saltwater crocodiles.

VS HIPPOPOTAMUS

Africa's most dangerous animal might look cuddly, but when this **herbivore** is hungry, look out! He's fast and furious on land and in the water, and may be responsible for killing 3,000 people per year!

Nickname:
The Muddy Maniac

Fatal Facts:
Hippos are famous for their hot tempers and will attack for the smallest reason.

Hippos sweat a red, sticky substance that acts as sun cream. People used to think it was blood!

GRUMPH!

BITE CLUB

It's the killer croc versus the hot-tempered hippo – which set of terrible teeth will win the title of champion chomper? Strongest bite wins!

Bite force is measured in pounds (lb) per square inch (psi).

(1 inch = 2.54 cm)

Crocodile Bite

PSI: 3700 lb

In a dramatic turn of events, the crocodile broke the stick!

Hippopotamus Bite

PSI: 1821 lb

(1 inch = 2.54 cm)

This bite feels like 1,821 pounds of weight on each inch it's pressing on!

Round two goes to the **saltwater crocodile!**

HALL OF FAME

Sydney Funnel-Web Spider
The world's most venomous spider.

Lives: Australia

Eats: Insects, small frogs and lizards

Deadly: Strong fangs can pierce leather

Mosquito
These bugs are harmless… unless they are carrying **malaria**.

Lives: Worldwide

Eats: Blood

Deadly: Kills 725,000 people each year

Blue-Ringed Octopus
A tiny bite with a nasty venom.

Lives: Australia

Eats: Crabs, shrimp and fish

Deadly: Has enough venom to kill 26 adult humans in a few minutes

Homo Sapiens
That's right; WE are the deadliest of all!

Lives: Worldwide

Eats: Farmed meat, vegetables and dairy

Deadly: Responsible for the extinction of many species, second biggest killer of humans in any year, global warming, nuclear weapons, and capable of destroying all life – we're pretty deadly

QUIZ AND...

You know whose bark is worse than their bite; see if you can get our quiz questions right...

Questions

1. Where do box jellyfish live?

2. How big can the geographer cone snail grow?

3. How many elephants could a single poison dart frog kill?

4. Which part of a black mamba is actually black?

5. How many people have been killed by saltwater crocodiles since 1976?

6. What special job does hippo sweat do?

Answers: 1. Northern Australia and the Indo-Pacific. 2. Up to 15 cm. 3. Two. 4. Its mouth. 5. 106. 6. It acts as sun cream.

... ACTIVITY

Play tag in the swimming pool – just like a box jellyfish!

Tag!

Brush your teeth twice a day so they are nice and strong, like the black mamba!

Throwing bean bags makes great target practice – just like the cone snail!

23

GLOSSARY

antivenom	a medicine used to treat poisons
gastropod	snails, slugs, cowries, whelks and limpets
herbivore	an animal that only eats plants
indigenous people	people originating from a particular place
malaria	a serious disease that causes chills, fever and sweating
marine	having to do with the sea
paralyse	cause something to be unable to move
predators	animals that eat other animals for food
species	a group of very similar animals or plants that are capable of producing young together
toxin	a poisonous substance

INDEX

Africa 7, 9, 13, 17
Australia 6–7, 20–21
blood 12, 17, 20
fangs 20

India 7
malaria 20
poison arrows 9
South America 6, 9

teeth 7, 16–19, 23
toxins 8–10